Amazing Animals
Polar Bears

Please visit our web site at www.garethstevens.com
For a free catalog describing our list of high-quality books, call 1-800-542-2595 (USA) or 1-800-387-3178 (Canada).
Our fax: 1-877-542-2596

Library of Congress Cataloging-in-Publication Data

Wilsdon, Christina.
   Polar Bears / by Christina Wilsdon.
        p. cm.—(Amazing Animals)
      Originally published: Pleasantville, NY: Reader's Digest Young Families, c2006.
      Includes bibliographical references and index.
      ISBN-10: 0-8368-9110-4   ISBN-13: 978-0-8368-9110-2 (lib. bdg.)
      ISBN-10: 1-4339-2027-1   ISBN-13: 978-1-4339-2027-1 (soft cover)
   1. Polar bear—Juvenile literature. I. Title.
QL737.C27W557 2009
599.786—dc22   2008027909

This edition first published in 2009 by
Gareth Stevens Publishing
A Weekly Reader® Company
1 Reader's Digest Road
Pleasantville, NY 10570-7000 USA

This edition copyright © 2009 by Gareth Stevens, Inc. Original edition copyright © 2006 by Reader's Digest Young Families, Pleasantville, NY 10570

Gareth Stevens Senior Managing Editor: Lisa M. Herrington
Gareth Stevens Creative Director: Lisa Donovan
Gareth Stevens Art Director: Ken Crossland
Gareth Stevens Associate Editor: Amanda Hudson
Gareth Stevens Publisher: Keith Garton

Consultant: Robert E. Budliger (Retired), NY State Department of Environmental Conservation

Photo Credits
Front cover: Dynamic Graphics, Inc.,Title page: Dynamic Graphics, Inc., Contents page: Photodisc/Getty Images, pages 6-7: Dynamic Graphics, Inc., page 8: Digital Vision, page 10: Courtesy of U.S. Fish and Wildlife Service, page 11: Brand X Pictures, page 12: Dynamic Graphics, Inc., pages 14-16: Digital Vision, page 19: Dynamic Graphics, Inc., page 20: Digital Vision, page 21: Dynamic Graphics, Inc., pages 22-23: Digital Vision, page 24: Corel Corporation, page 25: Dreamstime.com/ Anthony Hathaway, pages 27-29: Photodisc/Getty Images, pages 30-32: Dynamic Graphics, Inc., page 35: JupiterImages, page 36: Dynamic Graphics, Inc., pages 38-39: Dynamic Graphics, Inc., page 41: Digital Vision, page 43: Digital Vision, pages 44-45: Digital Vision, Back cover: Digital Vision.

Printed in the United States of America

1 2 3 4 5 6 7 8 9 13 12 11 10 09

Amazing Animals
Polar Bears

By Christina Wilsdon

Gareth Stevens
Publishing

Contents

Chapter 1
A Polar Bear Story

A female polar bear stretched her legs and yawned. She was eager to leave her den in the snow. She had been inside it since October. Now it was March—six months later! She could not wait to go outside.

But the bear had not been just napping in the den all winter. She had also given birth to two babies. That was why she had dug the den in the first place.

The mother bear's two little cubs were born in December. They were covered with a thin fuzz instead of fur and could not see or hear. She cuddled them close as they drank her rich milk.

Now the babies were busy, furry cubs that could see and hear. Each one weighed almost 30 pounds (14 kilograms)—about as much as a human two-year-old. The cubs were also ready to leave the den.

Ice Bears

The Inuit people of northern Canada call the polar bear *nanuk*, which means "ice bear."

At first, the cubs were afraid. They pressed close to their mother. The air felt cold. Bright light dazzled their eyes.

The mother bear was hungry. She had not eaten since October. She had lived off the fat in her body for all those months. But her fat supply was almost all gone now. She was ready to travel to the coast, where she could hunt for seals.

The cubs could not make this trip yet. They needed more time to get used to being outdoors in the cold. They also needed more time to strengthen their leg muscles.

So the bear family stayed close to the den for a few weeks. The cubs romped and wrestled. The three bears slept in hollows scraped out of the snow. They went back into the den only when there was a big storm.

Dig It!

A female polar bear digs her den in a heap of snow. The den usually faces south, toward the Sun, to add extra warmth. The body heat of the mother and her cubs also warms up the den.

Den Mothers

Female polar bears that are going to have babies are the only polar bears that spend winter in dens. Other polar bears continue to roam and hunt.

Biggest Bears

Polar bears are the biggest bears in the world—bigger even than grizzlies!

What a Meal!

A polar bear can eat as much as 100 pounds (45 kg) of food at one time.

One day, the mother bear turned to her cubs and made a coughing sound. It meant "Follow me!" Then she set out for the coast. The cubs stepped into the big paw prints she made. Sometimes they climbed onto their mother's back.

The mother bear had made this trip before. She knew that she would find seals along the coast. She knew the seals were giving birth to their pups in snow dens on the ice. She would show her cubs how to find these dens and catch the seals.

The cubs watched their mother hunt. But they also found time to play. The cubs chased each other through the snow. If they went too far, their mother called them back.

When it was time for the cubs to drink milk, their mother dug a hole in the snow, then sat in it as if it were an armchair. The cubs snuggled close to her.

The cubs will soon start eating meat. They will stop drinking milk. But they will not leave their mother. They will stay with her for another two years, learning how to be adult polar bears.

Chapter 2
The Body of a Polar Bear

Polar bears are the world's biggest meat-eating land animals!

Super Size

Polar bears live in the **Arctic**. The Arctic is a place of ice and snow at Earth's North Pole. In winter, temperatures drop far below freezing. Cold winds and snowstorms sweep the land. Trees cannot grow in the frozen soil. These treeless plains are called **tundra**.

Polar bears have changed, or **adapted**, to Arctic life. One adaptation is size. Big bodies lose heat more slowly than small bodies—and polar bears are huge! A male polar bear can weigh from 770 pounds to 1,500 pounds (349 to 680 kg)

When standing on all fours, a male polar bear is only about 4 feet (1.2 meters) high, but he's 10 feet (3 m) tall when he stands on his hind legs. A bear this tall would have to duck to go through a doorway without hitting his head! Females are about half the size of males.

Wedge Shape

A polar bear's body is shaped different than the bodies of other bears. A polar bear's head is longer and more pointed. Its neck is longer, too. This gives the bear a shape like a **wedge**. Being wedge-shaped helps a polar bear zoom through water when it swims.

A Furry Snowsuit

A polar bear is covered with fur except for its nose, lips, eyes, and the black pads on the bottom of its paws.

The color of a polar bear's fur helps it blend in with snow and ice. The outer fur is made up of long, hollow hairs called **guard hairs**. Although they look white, guard hairs have no color—they are clear. Like snow, guard hairs look white because they reflect sunlight. At sunrise and sunset, a polar bear may look pink or orange—or blue on a foggy day!

Guard hairs also help waterproof a bear. They are smooth, so water slides off them.

Under the guard hairs is a fuzzy layer of fur that helps hold warm air close to the body. The skin itself is black. This dark skin soaks up heat and light better than pale skin would. The black skin shows through on hairless parts of the bear, such as its nose and lips.

A layer of fat lies under the skin. A well-fed bear may have a fat layer that is 5 inches (13 centimeters) thick to help keep it warm.

Color Changes

A polar bear's fur often turns yellow or brown over time as it gets stained by meals of seal fat. Sunlight can also make fur yellow in much the same way that it yellows newspaper.

A polar bear is so warm inside its fur that it sometimes rolls in the snow to cool off!

Full of Fur

Just one square inch of a polar bear's skin can contain more than 9,000 hairs!

This is one square inch.

The fur on the bottom of a
polar bear's paws stops the
bear from sliding on ice and
snow. The black pads are
rough with tiny bumps.

Bigfoot Bears

A polar bear has huge feet. Each paw can be 12 inches (30 cm) wide!

Big feet are a useful adaptation to life in a land of snow and ice. They work like built-in snowshoes. They spread out the bear's weight so that it does not sink into snow or crash through ice. A polar bear may also shimmy across thin ice on its belly or on its elbows and knees to spread out its weight even more.

Having large paws also helps a polar bear swim. Its front paws are partly webbed between the toes. The webbing helps the paws work like flippers when the polar bear swims. The big back paws are used for steering.

Paws and Claws

Each polar bear paw is tipped with five long, hooked claws. The claws help a polar bear grip the ice. This is very useful when the polar bear climbs out of the water onto ice.

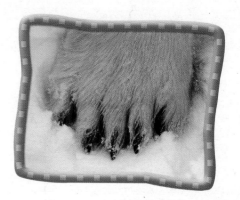

Chapter 3

Polar Bears on the Prowl

23

Polar bears are patient. They sometimes wait for hours at a seal's breathing hole for the seal to stick its head out.

Waiting for a Meal

The polar bear is a **predator**—an animal that eats other animals to survive. Its main **prey** is the ringed seal, but a polar bear will also eat other types of seals.

Ringed seals live in the Arctic Ocean. They spend lots of time underwater, but they must come up to breathe. So a ringed seal makes holes in the ice that covers the water. These holes are called **breathing holes**. A seal pops its head out of a breathing hole to get fresh air. It also enters and exits the water through these holes.

Polar bears know that if they sit and wait by a hole, a seal may pop up. This kind of hunting is called **still-hunting**.

A polar bear that is still-hunting first finds a hole. It can even sniff out a breathing hole that has been covered by a pile of snow.

Ringed seal

Then the bear settles by the hole to wait. It may sit down or lie on its belly, with its chin resting on the ice. Then it stays perfectly still. It doesn't move a muscle until a seal pokes its head out of the hole. Only then does the bear lunge! It grabs the seal and drags it onto the ice.

Hunting for a Meal

Piles of snow often drift over breathing holes. In spring, ringed seals carve dens into these drifts. Their pups rest in these dens. A polar bear can smell and hear a pup inside a den. The bear stands up on its hind legs. Then it smashes open the den with its front paws.

A polar bear also hunts by sneaking up on seals that are lying on the ice. When it gets very close, the polar bear charges at its prey. Sometimes the seal is able to escape by diving through a breathing hole.

A polar bear also sneaks up on resting seals by swimming. The bear paddles quietly up to the edge of the ice. Then it bursts out of the water to grab a seal.

Sea Bears

Polar bears are at home in the sea. In summer, they sometimes spend hours in the water just for fun! They can stay underwater for 2 minutes at a time and swim up to 40 miles (64 kilometers) without stopping!

Blubber Bears

Polar bears are the only bears that have **blubber**, a thick layer of fat under the skin. Blubber helps keep them warm in the Arctic's icy water and air.

Polar bears use their amazing sense of smell to find seals and other food.

A polar bear eats only the skin and fat of the seals it catches, which means there's lots left over for other creatures.

Polar Bear Meals

Polar bears depend on seals for most of their food, but they also eat other animals. Big polar bears prey on adult walruses. Smaller polar bears go after walrus pups. Polar bears sometimes catch white whales called belugas. This happens when belugas get trapped in a small patch of water surrounded by ice. The bears grab the whales and pull them out of the water.

Polar bears also eat fish, seabirds and their eggs, and any leftovers they find. They will travel for miles to feed on a dead whale lying onshore.

A polar bear does not eat every bit of the seals it catches. It usually eats only the seals' fat and skin. A polar bear would need lots more water to digest meat. The bear can't drink seawater because it is salty, and eating snow makes the bear too cold.

Leftover Luck

Arctic foxes follow polar bears. They eat any scraps that polar bears leave behind. Gulls and ravens also feed on polar bear meals. Young polar bears eat leftovers from the meals of older bears.

Arctic fox

Chapter 4
Polar Bears Together

Playtime for male polar bears sometimes means a wrestling match!

King of the Chill

Polar bears are loners. They do not live in groups or seek out other bears for company. But sometimes even polar bears must spend time with other bears.

Sometimes polar bears see one another when they are hunting for food. They may seem to form a group if many polar bears come to one place at the same time, but they are not together.

Male polar bears may ignore each other when they meet. But sometimes the two bears play. They stand on their hind legs and try to knock the other one down. The bears do not hurt each other in these fights.

Their play-fighting is practice for real battles. These battles take place during the mating season, which runs from April to May. Male bears fight over females during this time. They scratch and bite each other, sometimes leaving scars. Some males have so many scars from battles that they look like they have stripes!

Polar Places

A territory is a place that provides an animal with a home and food. Many animals will fight to defend their territory. Brown bears and black bears have territories, but polar bears do not. They just head for places where there are lots of seals.

Bear Pairs

A male polar bear uses his sense of smell to find a female bear. He tracks her down, sometimes for miles.

A female bear with cubs will not let a male bear near her. Male bears sometimes kill cubs. A female will attack a male to drive him away even before he comes close to her family.

But a female bear without cubs is ready to mate again in spring. Male bears for miles around know this. As many as six will arrive in her neighborhood at about the same time. They growl at each other and sometimes fight.

Finally, one male succeeds in chasing away the others. The female polar bear lets the winning male bear come near her. They spend a few days together. Then they part ways, each going back to live on its own.

When a Polar Bear Meets a Grizzly...

Polar bears and brown bears (grizzlies) sometimes mate. A cub that is half polar bear and half brown bear is often white when it is born. It may grow up to be brownish gray, pale yellow, or even white with brown patches.

A male and female polar bear nuzzle and sniff each other after the male has chased away any competitors.

Polar bear cubs take naps
just as human kids do.

Care Bears

The strongest bond between polar bears is between female bears and their cubs. Female polar bears are devoted moms. They watch their cubs carefully and warn them away from danger. They chase away male bears that might hurt the cubs. If cubs misbehave, their mother nips them or presses them against the ground.

Cubs spend their first year following their mother. They watch her and copy what she does. This is how they learn to hunt. Sometimes cubs get bored sitting quietly. They start playing and spoil their mother's still-hunting!

But cubs learn their hunting lessons over time. A one-year-old cub can catch a seal pup by itself. A two-year-old cub can wander away and catch bigger seals.

Most cubs stay with their mothers for two and a half years. They are big enough to take care of themselves by then. Cubs in one part of Canada spend just one and a half years with their mothers. Scientists are studying these bears to find out why.

Chapter 5
Polar Bears in the World

Lands of Ice and Snow

Polar bears live where it is cold most of the year and the ocean is covered with large sheets of ice, called **floes**. In fall, polar bears move from land to floes that form near shores. They look for seals in big cracks in the floes and for seals' breathing holes.

In spring, sea ice melts in southern parts of the polar bears' world. The bears travel farther north to find ice that is still solid.

In some places, all the sea ice melts, and polar bears must stay on land until the water freezes again.

Polar bears live mainly in the Arctic. The Arctic lies above a line marked on maps that is called the Arctic Circle. Trees do not grow above this line.

Polar bears live along Arctic coastlines in Canada, Russia, Greenland, and islands belonging to Norway and Russia. They also live in the United States, in Alaska.

Where Polar Bears Live

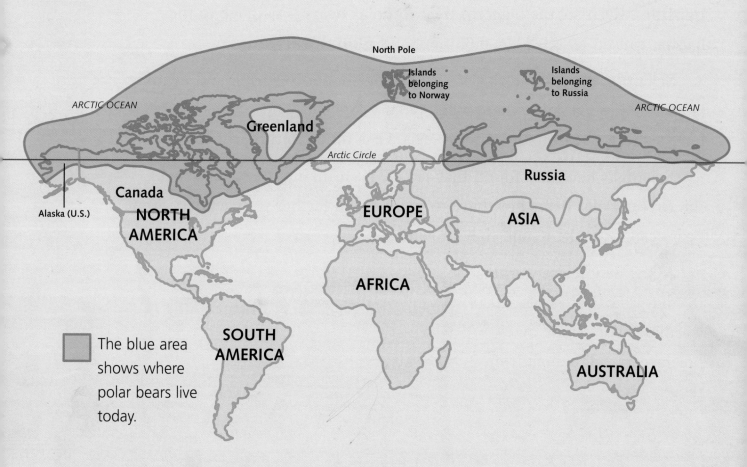

North Pole

Islands belonging to Norway

Islands belonging to Russia

ARCTIC OCEAN

ARCTIC OCEAN

Greenland

Arctic Circle

Russia

Alaska (U.S.)

Canada

NORTH AMERICA

EUROPE

ASIA

AFRICA

SOUTH AMERICA

AUSTRALIA

The blue area shows where polar bears live today.

The Future of Polar Bears

The polar bear's only predators are humans. Nations with polar bears signed The International Agreement on the Conservation of Polar Bears in 1973 to control hunting and to **conserve** and protect polar bear **habitats**. Even so, the biggest threat to polar bears is damage to their habitat caused by oil spills, pollution, and **global warming**.

Scientists have found that ice is melting sooner in spring and forming later in fall in Canada, where many polar bears live. This means the bears have a shorter season for hunting seals. Less time often means less food.

Scientists have also found that sea ice is shrinking in other parts of the Arctic. Polar bears now have to swim much farther to reach ice. Some bears cannot make it, and they drown.

Many people are working to find ways to slow global warming. They hope that polar bears will benefit from their work.

Fast Facts About Polar Bears

Scientific name	*Ursus maritimus*
Class	Mammalia
Order	Carnivora
Weight	Males to 1,500 pounds (680 kg) Females to 880 pounds (399 kg)
Life span	15-18 years in the wild 30 years in captivity
Habitat	Arctic tundra and pack ice
Top speed	25 miles per hour (40 km/h)

Save Energy, Save the Polar Bear

You can help preserve polar bears and their Arctic habitat by saving energy in your home. Here are four easy ways:

- Put on a sweater instead of turning up the heat.
- Turn off TVs and computers when you're not using them.
- Recycle cans, bottles, paper, and other items.
- Take a quick shower instead of a bath.

Water Bears

Because polar bears spend so much time in ocean waters, scientists call them marine mammals. The word *marine* means "about the sea."

The polar bear's scientific name, *Ursus maritimus*, means "sea bear" in Latin.

Glossary

adaptation — a change over time in an animal's body or behavior that helps it survive in its habitat

Arctic — northern lands and oceans where it is cold and snowy much of the year

blubber — a thick layer of fat under the skin that helps keep an animal warm

boar — a male bear

breathing hole — a hole that a seal digs through the ice to use as an entrance and exit as well as for coming up for air

conserve — to protect and preserve land, animals, plants, and other natural resources

cub — a baby bear

floes — sheets of ice on the ocean

global warming — a rise in the average temperature of the Earth's atmosphere that causes a change in climate

guard hairs — long hairs that form the outer layer of a polar bear's fur

habitat — the natural environment where an animal or a plant lives

predator — an animal that hunts and eats other animals to survive

prey — animals that are eaten by other animals

sow — a female bear

still-hunting — a way of hunting that involves sitting still and waiting by a seal's breathing hole

tundra — a big area of land in the Arctic region with no trees and a permanently frozen layer of soil

wedge — something that is thick at one end and thin at the other

Polar Bears: Show What You Know

How much have you learned about polar bears? Grab a piece of paper and a pencil and write your answers down.

1. How does it help a polar bear to have a wedge-shaped body?

2. What is the main food of polar bears?

3. Why do polar bears have a layer of blubber underneath their skin?

4. What is the name for the type of hunting polar bears use near seal breathing holes?

5. Why do polar bears usually eat only the skin and fat of seals?

6. Why do mother polar bears stay away from male bears?

7. How long do most polar bear cubs stay with their mothers?

8. What are the large ice sheets that polar bears travel on called?

9. What is the biggest threat to the future of polar bears?

10. Why do scientists call polar bears marine mammals?

1. The shape helps it zoom through the water when it swims. 2. Seals—especially ringed seals 3. To help keep them warm 4. Still-hunting 5. Because they would need extra water to digest the meat 6. Because male bears sometimes kill cubs 7. Two and a half years 8. Floes 9. Damage to their habitat caused by oil spills, pollution, and global warming 10. Because they spend so much time in the water

For More Information

Books

Face to Face With Polar Bears. Face to Face With Animals (series). Rosing, Norbert (National Geographic Children's Books, 2007)

Knut: How One Little Polar Bear Captured the World. Hatkoff, Craig (Scholastic, 2007)

Polar Bears and the Arctic. Magic Tree House Research Books (series). Osborne, Mary Pope (Random House, 2007)

Web Sites

National Geographic Kids: Polar Bears

www.kids.nationalgeographic.com/Animals/CreatureFeature/Polar-bear

Be sure to check out all the fun activities on this informative site, including a free card you can send to your friends.

Polar Bears International

www.polarbearsinternational.org

Find lots of amazing photos and plenty of fun facts on this site devoted to conserving polar bear habitats.

Index